A SELF-LOVE JOURNAL

100 Things
I about
ME

Tanaya Winder

R

ROCKRIDGE
PRESS

First Rockridge Press hardcover edition 2022

Originally published in trade paperback by Rockridge Press 2021

Rockridge Press and the Rockridge Press logo are trademarks or registered trademarks of Callisto Media Inc. and/or its affiliates in the United States and other countries and may not be used without written permission.

For general information on our other products and services, please contact our Customer Care Department within the United States at (866) 744-2665, or outside the United States at (510) 253-0500.

Hardcover ISBN: 979-8-88608-588-4 | Paperback ISBN: 978-1-63807-333-8

Manufactured in the United States of America.

Series Designer: Liz Cosgrove
Interior and Cover Designer: Scott Petrower
Art Producer: Sara Feinstein
Editor: Samantha Holland
Production Editor: Nora Milman
Production Manager: Michael Kay

Illustrations used under license from Shutterstock.com.

10 9 8 7 6 5 4 3 2 1 0

This journal belongs to

....

Author's Note

Welcome! I'm so excited for you to use this journal. As an artist, writer, and educator, I've helped steward many people on their journeys of self-discovery. Self-love is one of my favorite forms of love. Self-love can be as simple as taking time for yourself. It can be as easy as acknowledging that you need sleep and allowing yourself to rest. Self-love can also be work; giving yourself time to reflect isn't always easy, but the process is always worth it. No matter where you are in your life, it is never too late to work on deepening your relationship with yourself. I have no doubt you will discover more than 100 things that you love about yourself. Be open, be honest, and allow yourself to be vulnerable on the page. I hope these exercises, reminders, and tips offer you a road map to remembering all the things you love about yourself and more.

With love,
Tanaya

1.

Self-love is a daily practice.

Today, I'll practice

....

2.

I admire the way I ....

and ....

YOU
LOOK
GREAT

3.

To me, success means

....

Self-Love Reminder

You were born with a purpose, and part of life is figuring out what that purpose is. Remember what makes you light up. Remember your passion. Remember what makes you feel most alive.

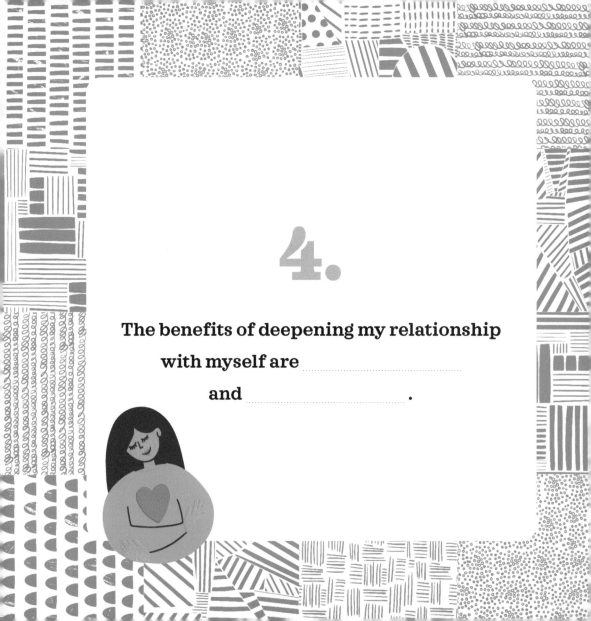

4.

The benefits of deepening my relationship with myself are .... and ....

5.

I am passionate about ....

and ....

6.

I am the best version of myself when I

7.

I tap into my strength and inner power when . . .

....

....

Self-Love Tip

Put your feet on the floor or ground and anchor yourself. Stand tall and feel yourself rising from your roots. Wiggle your toes and feel yourself awakening from your feet to the top of your head. Stretch your hands up toward the sun and sky. What do you notice happening in your body? Remember this feeling when you need to be reminded what it feels like to stretch into new areas of your life.

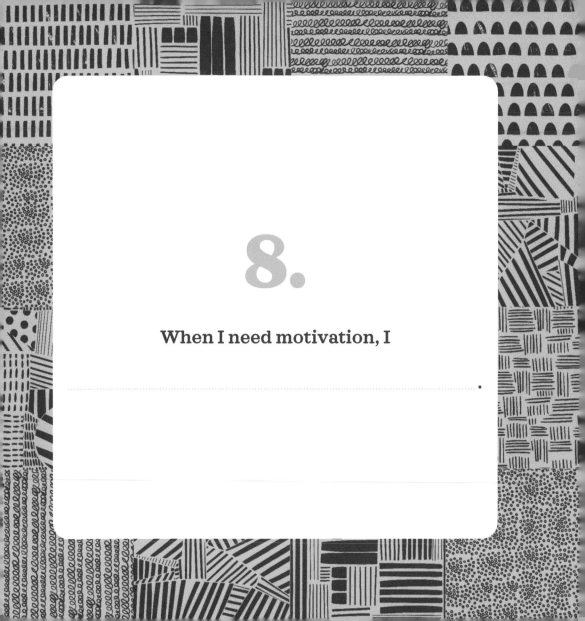

8.

When I need motivation, I

9.

I feel valued when my friends
and loved ones tell me

10.

My favorite forms of self-care are
and   .

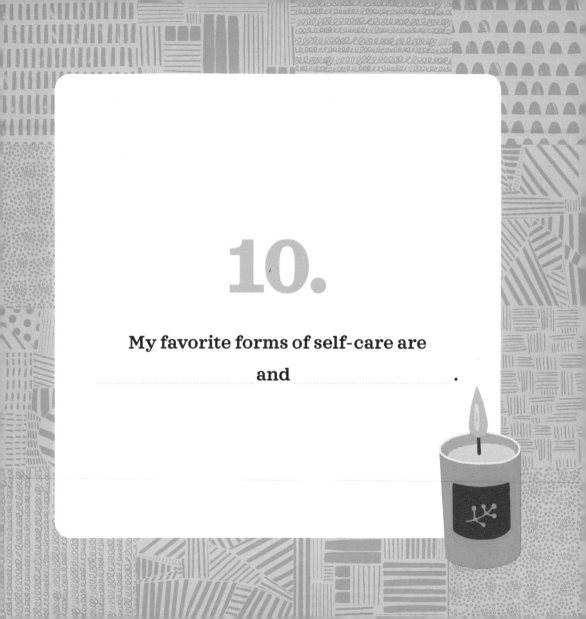

Self-Love Reminder

Be patient with yourself on your journey. There will be successes and there may be struggles. Just remember you already have everything you need to take control of your path. You've got this!

11.

Today, I will forgive myself for

....

12.

Your values help form your foundation. What values (respect, honesty, empathy, trust, etc.) do you hold tightly to when making decisions? Write about the values that make you who you are.

....

....

....

....

....

13.

**Whether it's personal or professional,
I know I am valued when**

....

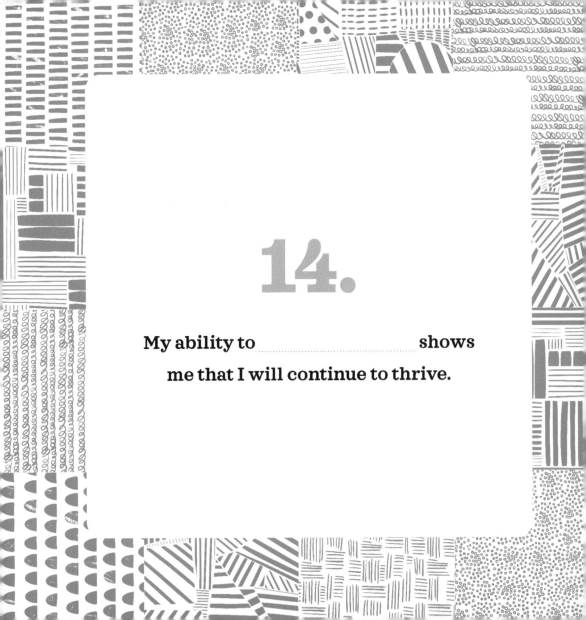

14.

My ability to .... shows me that I will continue to thrive.

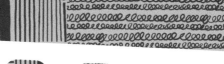

Self-Love Tip

When your mind is racing and you're thinking about a million things, relax yourself by staying in the moment. Be present and reconnect with yourself. Look around you and take inventory of your surroundings. What are three things you see, two things you hear, and one thing you smell?

15.

**If I don't feel good enough,
I will remind myself that**

....

16.

One of the best days I can remember was when . . .

17.

My happy space always includes

.... **and** ....

Self-Love Reminder

Give yourself permission to shine brightly, embrace your gifts, and live life to the fullest.

18.

The positive statement I want to share with myself today is:

. . . .

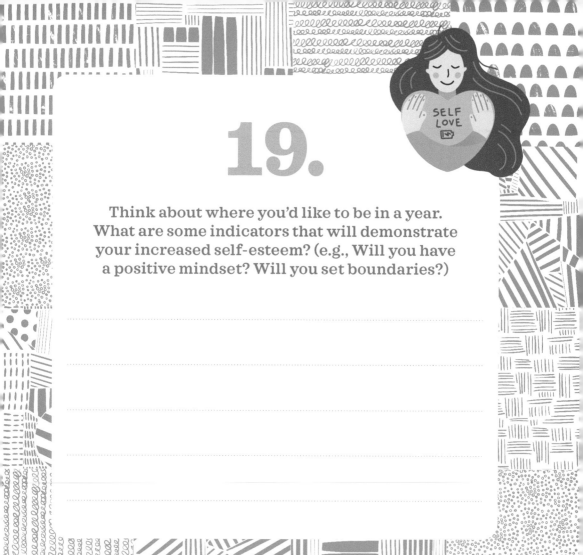

19.

Think about where you'd like to be in a year. What are some indicators that will demonstrate your increased self-esteem? (e.g., Will you have a positive mindset? Will you set boundaries?)

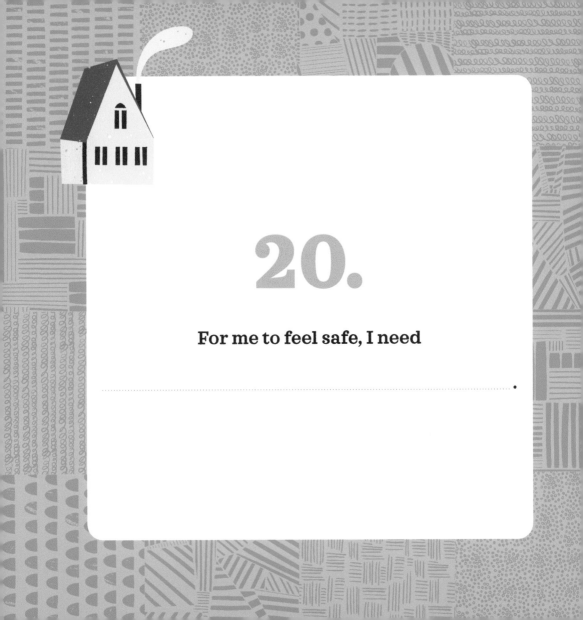

20.

For me to feel safe, I need

Self-Love Tip

When you need grounding, sit or lie in a comfortable position and close your eyes. Relax your entire body, rest your arms at your side, or place your palms on your heart—whatever feels right to you. Practice deep breathing. As you breathe in, visualize bringing light into your body. As you breathe out, let go of stress and exhale any negative thoughts. When you breathe in again, visualize your breath as a light that you're sending to every part of your body that needs healing or love.

21.

When you were younger, what did you believe was important about self-love? What are your self-love goals today? Are there any similarities or differences?

....

....

....

....

....

22.

I was tested when I _____,
but I overcame it by _____.

23.

I remember this one time
I .... It was awesome!

24.

I feel seen when someone tells me

Self-Love Tip

When critical thoughts about yourself enter your mind, do a quick check-in. Ask yourself: "Does this thought serve me?" If it's a negative thought about yourself, acknowledge the thought, thank it for paying a visit, then let it go. It helps to visualize thoughts as balloons. Let the negative ones go. Hold on to those positive thoughts because they do serve you. They contribute to your deepening of your relationship with yourself.

25.

I show myself love by .... ,

.... , and ....

26.

I will be patient with myself when I

....

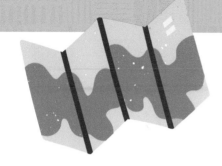

27.

When I feel lost, I know _____
and _____ will ground me.

Self-Love Tip

Remember that self-love is an ongoing process. It's okay to experience some setbacks. You're human and a complex individual. You are a whole person with a lifetime of experiences to draw on. Close your eyes and embrace gratitude. As you breathe in and out, visualize some things you are grateful for.

28.

I saw myself in a new and positive way when . . .

.

29.

I am grateful for ....

and ....

30.

Once, I thought I made a big mistake
when I _____ , but then
I realized I learned _____ .

Self-Love Tip

If you feel overwhelmed or anxious, shut off all your electronic devices. Turn off the TV or computer, and silence or turn off your phone. In this fast-paced digital world, we can get bombarded with news, social media, and ads. Turn off and tune out so you can tune in to what is going on in your mind and heart. Take a walk, practice deep breathing, and visualize what nourishes you.

31.

My favorite way of showing love is through

....

32.

My favorite way of receiving love is by

....

33.

When I _____ , I knew
I was capable of pursuing my goals.

34.

I celebrate all my wins. One small
win I had this week was

Self-Love Reminder

What you're doing is enough. You don't have to be perfect. You don't always have to be the best. Just try your best. You were always enough. You *are* always enough.

35.

When reflecting on your journey, what experiences come to mind? Write about some things you want to remember so that when you look back through this journal, you'll be reminded of your path.

....

....

....

....

....

36.

My strength comes from my

....

37.

When I feel like I am not enough,
I will remind myself that I am

....

Self-Love Reminder

You have a voice, and that voice is worth sharing in a genuine way. Keep yourself open to new chapters; your story is still unfolding.

38.

_____ reminds
me that I can do anything.

39.

When my friends and/or loved ones

.... , I know that I am loved.

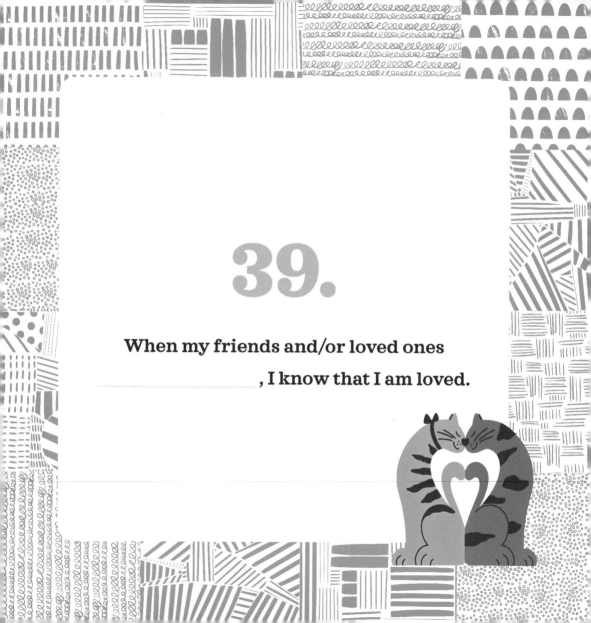

40.

When I achieve one of my goals, I feel

.

Self-Love Tip

Think about what nourishes life. For instance, you know that a plant needs water and sunlight to grow. How can you apply those needs to your life? Get outside, soak in some sun, and drink plenty of water. Give yourself the nourishment you need.

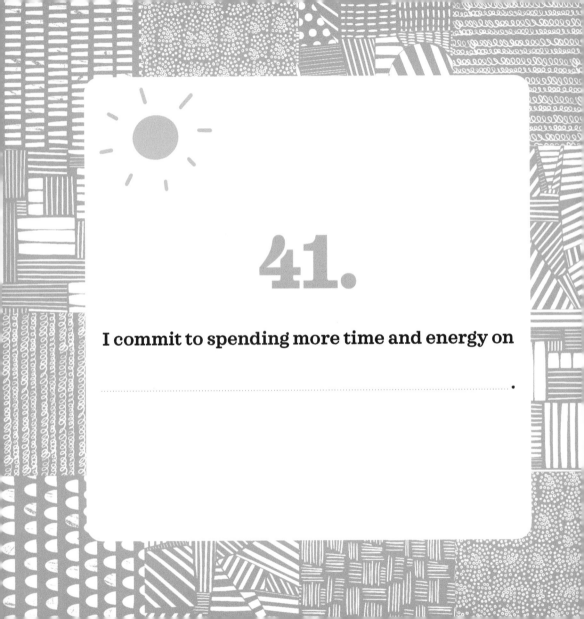

41.

I commit to spending more time and energy on

.

42.

I felt proud of myself when I . . .

....

....

43.

Three things that bring me joy are

.... , ... ,

and ....

44.

Today, I will allow myself to just be. Self-care for me means

....

....

....

45.

**I feel like I can harness my power when
I** .... **,** .... **,
and** .... **.**

46.

Think about someone who has helped impact who you are today. Write them a thank-you note.

....

....

....

....

....

....

Self-Love Tip

The words you say about yourself and your life, whether positive ("I've got this! I'm good enough.") or negative ("I don't deserve this."), have the power to impact your mindset. The words you say to yourself impact your inner being. Put your hands on your heart, close your eyes, take a deep breath, and repeat aloud, "I am worthy. I am safe. I belong. I matter. I am loved."

47.

I am grateful for my body. It allows me to

_____ and _____ .

48.

I can't help but laugh at myself when I . . .

....

....

49.

I feel confident in my worth when

....

50.

Tomorrow, I will shift my perspective to be

.

51.

When I am challenged, I will remember

....

52.

I felt really brave when I . . .

. . . .

. . . .

53.

I inspire myself when I

....

LOVE INK

54.

Write a letter to your present self from your future self. What advice would you give?

....

....

....

....

....

....

55.

Three things I love about myself are

.... , ... ,

and ....

Self-Love Tip

Think of your calm place. What does it look like?
What do you see? Smell? Hear? Envision yourself
there and practice your deep breathing. Keep
that calm place in your heart when you're feeling
stressed or overwhelmed.

56.

When I'm feeling frustrated,

it helps to think of

....

57.

I know I am enough because

....

58.

I feel most at peace when

....

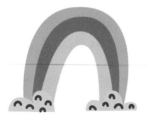

59.

My win for the day was...

....

....

60.

I show gratitude to myself when I

.... •

61.

My favorite part of my body is my

.

62.

The best part about how I love myself is the way I ⟍⟍⟍⟍⟍⟍⟍⟍⟍⟍⟍⟍ and ⟍⟍⟍⟍⟍⟍⟍⟍⟍⟍⟍⟍ .

63.

Remember a time you pushed yourself out of your comfort zone. What did it feel like? What do you appreciate about that experience?

....

....

....

....

....

64.

I love that people notice
_____ about me.

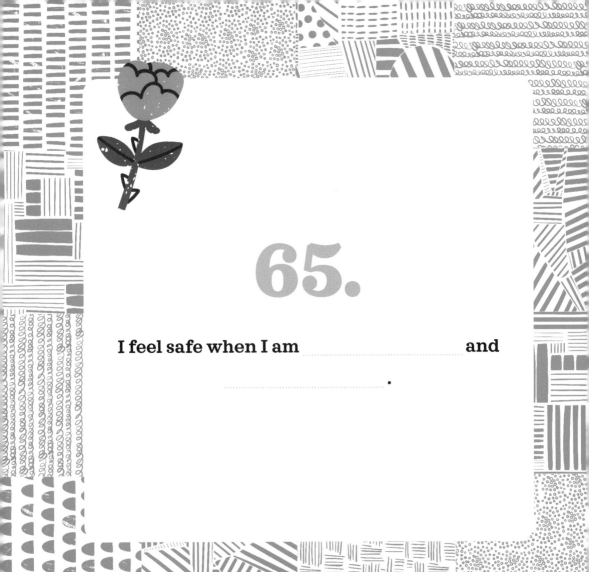

65.

I feel safe when I am .... **and**

....

66.

I love the way my brain works. No one sees
the same way I do.

Self-Love Reminder

Setting boundaries is one form of self-love. Remember that it's okay to prioritize your needs. To set your day with intention, ask yourself, "What do I need today?"

67.

When I enter a room, I bring _____ and _____ into the space.

68.

The deeper in love I fall with myself, the more I appreciate my ....

69.

When I need to be reminded that I
matter, I look myself in the mirror
and say, "I am .... ,
.... , and ...."

70.

When I think about shining moments in my life, one experience that comes to mind is . . .

71.

When I _____ and
_____ , I choose happiness.

72.

I no longer blame myself for
.... ; instead, I celebrate
the way I ....

73.

Even when it feels like no one is on
my side, I know that people

. ⋯⋯⋯⋯⋯⋯⋯⋯⋯⋯⋯⋯⋯⋯⋯⋯⋯⋯⋯⋯⋯⋯⋯⋯⋯⋯⋯

Self-Love Tip

Oftentimes when stressful things happen, you start thinking about all the other moments you felt stressed, not good enough, tested, etc. It can almost feel like you're caught in a downward shame spiral. Take a deep breath, pause, and tell yourself that you are not your mistakes. You are not the same person you were before. Remind yourself of how far you've come to get here to this person who is growing and becoming.

74.

When it comes to self-love, I am already good
at .... and ....

75.

Reflect on what's keeping you from being your full, authentic self. In the space below, acknowledge those emotions and write about what would happen if you let them go.

76.

Today, I release my fear of

and   .

77.

I appreciate the road I've traveled.
I respect my past self for

....

78.

I choose not to let negative thoughts control me. Today, I take control by

....

79.

I show love and appreciation to my body by
.... and ....

80.

When I
·····································,
I knew I was in my element.

81.

When I allow myself to love myself fully, I am

....

82.

I believe in myself because I: .... ,
.... , and ....

Self-Love Reminder

Each day is a new opportunity to continue on your path or try something new. Remind yourself that those opportunities are yours to take. Know that your goals are within your reach.

83.

I am learning to love and respect myself each day. Today, I send love to these parts of me: .... , ... , and ....

84.

If I had a feel-good playlist, some of the songs I'd add would be .... , ... , and ....

85.

The last time I laughed really hard was when . . .

.

86.

At the end of the day, what matters is that I

.

87.

Write about a noteworthy experience that helped show you more of who you are meant to be.

88.

Even when I'm _____, I still know I am worthy and deserving of love.

89.

I love when people notice the way I

....

90.

The truth I tell myself is that I am

....

91.

My self-care mission for this month is to

.

Self-Love Reminder

You know who you are and all the obstacles you've faced. Look back and take in all that you've overcome. Let this energy push you forward into what you want to triumph over next.

92.

One experience that pushed me
to grow was when . . .

93.

I used to think my limits

were ...., but I overcame

them by ....

94.

Today, I am sending love to these parts of my body: ……………………… ,
……………………… , and ……………………… .

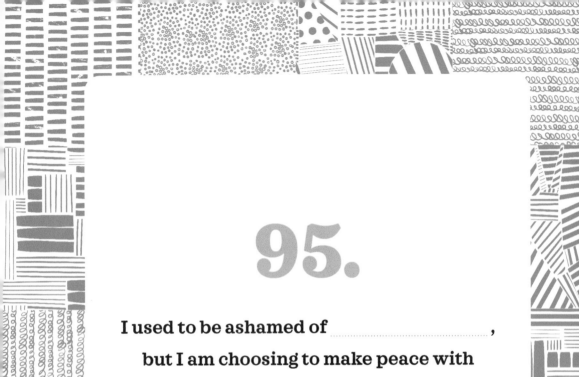

95.

I used to be ashamed of .... ,
but I am choosing to make peace with
everything that made me who I am today.

96.

Identify a fear that you have when it comes to pursuing your dreams. Write a breakup letter to that fear, telling it that it no longer has power over you.

97.

If someone I loved was going through what I'm experiencing right now, I would tell them

....

98.

I trust myself to make good decisions. One
decision I am proud of myself for is

....

99.

I felt empowered when . . .

....

....

100.

The only person I'll compare myself with
is myself. And I've learned how to

Self-Love Reminder

You are right where you are supposed to be.
You are here, breathing, alive, and on a journey
toward deepening your relationship with yourself.
Remember, you are worthy of taking this time
for yourself.